Happy in Spite of People

Ellen Castro's warm and witty book welcomes you to the feline world of Mr. P and its many colorful cats who will surely remind you of people you know. As the wise and spiritually-enlightened Mr. P tries to be a friend and coach to the frightened and the narcissistic, the aggressive and the depressed, he has much to teach readers about being at peace with themselves, their Creator and some of the challenging characters who come into all our lives.

Dr. Lee Bolman
Co-author of *Leading with Soul* and *Reframing Organizations*
The Marion H. Bloch, University of Missouri Chair in Leadership

Reading this book allowed me to see myself and others at different stages, to reflect on life experiences and to move ahead with peace of mind. A must read.

Jesse J. Tyson
Director, Global Aviation
ExxonMobil Petroleum and Chemical

"Happy in Spite of People" is a must read for all who wish to thrive in business and to enjoy life. Through Ellen's sincere and light-hearted coaching parable, readers are given practical applications that can be implemented immediately for living an inspired and authentic life.

Paula Hill Strasser
Director, Business Leadership Center, Edwin L. Cox School of Business
Southern Methodist University

This book is fantastic! I have read numerous self-help and leadership books, and none has impacted my business and personal life more quickly or positively than "Happy in Spite of People." I could identify with all the characters and learned a great deal about myself and others through these memorable stories. I plan to share this book with my family, friends and co-workers and to thrive through the lessons learned.

Troy Dawson
Director, ERP Systems
Microtune Inc.

I am not sure which cat I am, but I know I am more than one cat. Every employee, manager and executive will recognize themselves in "Happy in Spite of People." This is a great manual that converts complex characters to simpler traits that are easier to recognize and to understand. It also gives practical advice on handling these traits more effectively while being true to you. I know I will be rereading this book every time I meet new people to get quick, insightful tips on how to better deal with their personalities.

Inna Kizenkova
Vice President, Supplier Commerce EMEA
Sabre Holdings

Ellen Castro has created a personal and business guide for thriving, not just surviving in these volatile times. It is uniquely delivered as a cats' tale. Glance, reference or study, everyone can recognize the characters and will welcome her personal insights and advice – an excellent resource for building relationships of trust with others and oneself. A fantastic read!

Ashley Gold
Vice President and Customer Unit Head Vodafone Mumbai
Ericsson

"Happy in Spite of People" is a great antidote for the fears and insecurities of today's workplace. I enjoyed reading its many lessons about working with people who are challenged with the baggage of their prior mistakes and disappointments. "Happy in Spite of People" is also a gentle parable that explores the meaning of self-acceptance, proving once again that every day is a blessing, filled with new opportunities for connections with others.

Rita G. Ransdell
Vice President, Human Resources
American Airlines Center

Look out T.S. Eliot because Andrew Lloyd Webber has new material for a follow-up to "Cats." I can testify that Ellen's prestigious educational credentials and professional experience have been very effective while using her services at several of my companies. But with "Happy in Spite of People" she has taken that knowledge and presented it a meaningful way deeper than the words on the page. You know these people, and Ellen provides insightful and useful information to help you herd these "cats." It is the source for you on many levels: personally, professionally and spiritually.

Tom Waring
CEO
Trailblazer Studios

Ellen Castro uses a simple parable to share incredible wisdom about success in life and at work. It's uncomfortable to recognize ourselves in some of the cats. But we can take heart that, although we may have fewer than nine lives, we still have time to create better relationships with others and ourselves.

Lorri Allen
TV and Radio Personality

In these challenging times when nothing ever seems enough, "Happy in Spite of People" offers a solution. This fun and easy-to-read parable releases you from pressures and fears. It guides you to becoming more relaxed and enjoying life while being more productive and successful. This refreshing book is for everyone who wants to make a change and thrive both personally and professionally. Simply to be here and happy in spite of people.

Kristian Toivo
Chief Technology Officer and Vice President, Global Account Vodafone
Ericsson

Once again, Ellen comes up with a truly unique and fun approach to customer service. This is a great resource for our team to deliver exceptional customer service to our guests with a genuine smile. It'll also be an integral part of our new employee orientation to stimulate discussions!

Ben C. Danielsen
Director of Operations, Newbury, England
The Vineyard Group

It is often said that 'art imitates life.' In this case it is the lives of felines that paint the pathway of the complexities and challenges we face today. Ellen has taken as the backdrop a courageous central character, Mr. P.

In one sitting you will laugh, recall both the good and challenging times in your life, and finally reflect upon the potential we all have to shape our legacy by having a positive impact on the lives of others!

Billy E. Johnson
Executive, Human Resources

"Happy in Spite of People" showed me that I can be lifted to a higher reflection of myself and those around me when I understand that our personalities, like those of the cats, are shaped by our past and our inner level of conviction and self-confidence.

Becky Munoz-Diaz
Vice President and General Manager
Univision/Tele-Futura 49

You can reach higher peaks when you lighten the load. "Happy in Spite of People" enables the reader to remove the weight of having to gain the acceptance of others with self-acceptance. The result is achieving greater heights and living from your true calling. I will read this book again and again.

Bobby Vance
Sales Consultant
Park Place Motors

"Happy in Spite of People" is an engaging, insightful and delightful read that lifts the readers' mood and spirits. With every turn of the page, the reader gains fresh insights and perspective. It captures your attention and imagination for a better life from the beginning.

Julie Daugherty
National Accounts Manager
The PACE Organization Inc.

Project management is always about achieving results through others. "Happy in Spite of People" provides a roadmap for dealing effectively with the multiple personalities we experience while providing understanding of our own tendencies that impact the outcomes of our Projects – whether they are failures or successes.

While the parable will have you laughing out loud at times, the insights and practical applications are serious business and are real. They will help you to matrix back to your Team(s) Roles and Responsibilities in Projects for more success.

Pete H. Martinez
Past President Board of Directors PMI – Houston and Program Manager
Avaya

Ellen Castro captures her global consulting experiences, life experiences and educational background in "Happy in Spite of People." This informative, upbeat and motivational book captures and clearly summarizes many of the personalities that each of us deals and copes with daily. Her coaching advice is practical and pragmatic. When applied, it will assist the reader in having fewer conflicts and more meaningful relationships immediately.

Leigh Kohnfelder
Parent and Business Owner
Obsidian

"Happy in Spite of People" is a thought-provoking and engaging read. I love it! Through its humorous yet real life situations, readers can improve their business results. I plan to give a copy to all my staff.

Nancy Fossee
President and CEO
Fossee's

"Happy in Spite of People" is a charming journey through your inner feelings as well as most of the people you might know. Everyone you might interact with is represented in the characters. Mr. P is a delight and worth imitating. This parable is a very helpful guide for just about everyone. Thank you, Ms. Castro.

Cecilia McKay
Community Volunteer

This is a required leadership guide for everyone who is responsible for developing others and managing a team. Practical and concise, "Happy in Spite of People" is especially useful in today's economic and time-challenged environment.

Penny Schob
Senior Account Executive
Diebold

This is a lovely and truly captivating book. Ellen Castro and Mr. P take us through a journey of life lessons from the heart. It is a unique and magical story, written not just for cat lovers, but especially for anyone who loves life.

Homero Rivas, M.D., M.B.A., F.A.C.S.
Department of Surgery Assistant Professor
UT Southwestern Medical Center

This priceless parable doesn't need nine lives to speak to both heart and intellect. It has a life of its own and provokes a moving response for the reader. Through her cast of cat characters, Ellen blends the purr-fect combination of wisdom, humor, love and self-experience. The story is 'littered' with bits of entertaining information and practical experiences.

Ellen, like Mr. P, is at peace in her own fur and voicing her own 'purr.' She sees herself in everyone and shares willingly. Ellen gets readers to 'paws' and think in a whole new way. Her work on trust, choice, thriving and being present is furr-ociously witty and smart!

Kimberle Farver
Enterprise Consultant
HP/EDS

"Happy in Spite of People" will put a smile on your face as you read about the characters that are in all of our lives, and most importantly,

the different aspects of us as individuals. This book nourishes the soul by teaching about building confidence and trust. Thank you, Ellen, for writing a parable that we can all relate to.

Deborah Singlelton
Executive Director
Arasini Foundation

Through the characters in "Happy in Spite of People," I couldn't help but see people I know. I learned some new ways to respond to them more productively. The surprising part of this easy read was that is brought to my consciousness how my actions may affect others. The book is amazing.

Julie Hamrick
President and CEO
Ignite Sales Inc.

As I began reading the manuscript of "Happy in Spite of People," not being certain of the use of feline characters to illustrate various personalities and life's lessons, I didn't think I would enjoy the story. However, the more I read and the more I saw every person I have ever known in the characters, the more I enjoyed the reading. I didn't put it down until I finished. Everyone who reads these stories will learn something about themselves and about interacting with others. This is a must read! Call Oprah!!

Judge Ernie Glenn
Bexar County Felony Drug Court

HAPPY
in Spite of People

Ellen Castro
Chief Energizing Officer

Happy in Spite of People - Copyright © 2015 Ellen Castro

All rights reserved. No part of this publication may be reproduced, stored in a retrieval system, or transmitted, in any form or by any means, electronic, mechanical, photocopying, recording, or otherwise, without the prior written permission of the author.
All quotes appearing in *Happy in Spite of People* have been collected by the author over the years from various books.

ISBN: 0986349909
ISBN 13: 9780986349904
Library of Congress Control Number: 2015907142
Igniting Works, Dallas, TX, USA

IgnitingWorks@nimbleworldwide.com

Illustration by Subratta Dutta
Cover Design by nimble worldwide

Thank you, Rose and Tom Waring, for dropping priceless Mr. P on my doorstep.

To God be the Glory!

Table of Contents

Preface xvi
Introduction: Why a Parable? xx
Know Your Cats xxv

The Cats

Chapter 1	Mr. P, The Cat-Alyst	2
Chapter 2	Hoover, The Narcissist	7
Chapter 3	Peekaboo, The Timid Cat	12
Chapter 4	Bondo, The Fixer	18
Chapter 5	Bruiser, The Alpha Cat	24
Chapter 6	Scarlett, The Drama Queen	29
Chapter 7	Willow, The Pleaser	34
Chapter 8	Lucky, The Happy Cat	40
Chapter 9	Harvey, The Wounded Cat	44
Chapter 10	Luci, The Instigator	50
Chapter 11	Esperanza, The Harmonizer	54
Chapter 12	Chen, The Trusted Advisor	59

Coaching in the Park

Chapter 13	Clash of the Egos	66
Chapter 14	Unwound and Unlimited	71
Chapter 15	Living Your Joy	75
Chapter 16	You Can Always Choose Again	79
Chapter 17	Abra-Cat-Abra	83
Chapter 18	Hugs for Thugs	87
Chapter 19	Here and Happy	93
Chapter 20	Epilogue – Fur Now	96

Dare to be a Greater You! 98

Unstuck and Unlimited 101

Preface

*There are only two ways to live your life.
One as though nothing is a miracle.
The other is as though
everything is a miracle.*

— ALBERT EINSTEIN

The "age of disillusionment" is becoming more prevalent according to *The New York Times*. Weariness and spiritual poverty which impact the wealthy, the poor, the famous and everyone in between is on the rise with our fast paced, fascinating times. Add that to the reality that competence is no longer enough to succeed in business or in life, emotional intelligence is required – yikes!

The solutions for "disillusionment" and knowing how to get along with others are found in *Happy in Spite of People*. Happiness is an inside job. We are 100% responsible for our state of mind which impacts our state of life. When we are right and at peace with ourselves, everything seems like a miracle. Getting along with others is simply a by-product of our self-acceptance. We have been given a tremendous gift – the gift of choice – and a change in attitude changes everything.

Why be disillusioned? You were made on purpose for a purpose. You are one-of-a-kind! Life is for you. Even the pain has a purpose; it helps us develop character, strength and resiliency, if we choose. We can choose to be on society's treadmill of "it's never enough" and try filling the gaping hole in our souls with stuff, or choose to fill it with self-acceptance and self-love. I've tried both, and the latter two last!

How do I know? Experience is quite a teacher. Once upon a time, my issues had issues. I walked around with a thick armor of emotional scars and pink combat boots because life was a struggle and a fight for survival. I lived on high-alert most of my life based on a very interesting childhood. My mom was bipolar, nerve-racking and a walking time-bomb who committed suicide. My dad was a raging alcoholic perhaps due to feeling abandoned at age 17 when his beloved mother took her life. My grandfather was sexually abusive and his wife, Louise, thought I looked "too Mexican." While I had an outward bravado, I was dying inside.

The good news is that I am a fighter. After earning bachelor's and master's degrees in business, and battering my head on the glass ceiling in the oil industry for 5 promotions in 11 years, I enrolled at Harvard University at age 38 to pursue a graduate degree in education. But I was still the walking wounded, deeply depressed and thinking about suicide. I chose to visit the campus counselor for guidance and direction. After recounting the details of childhood and corporate experience, the counselor looked at me and said, "So you are letting a raging alcoholic define you. You are crazy." The epiphany!

"Change your thoughts to change your world" became my motto. I am more than my DNA, my past or environment. My choices define me. And with new found courage, a leap of faith and realizing I was a walking miracle, I began my path to becoming an empowering author, a trusted global consultant and coach to thousands. Just call me blessed. I broke through to the other side, from darkness and disillusionment to light and fulfillment!

We are all a bit wounded. We all have stories. However, we are *not* our stories. We all have choices. We can choose to be the victim or the victor if we have the courage to look at our lives. *We are far more powerful than we imagine.* I wrote *Happy in Spite of People* to give you a safe and gentle path to self-discovery and self-mastery, led by cats who deliver life messages and ease the struggles and tensions of interpersonal relationships. I pray the parable opens your heart to the possibilities of just how wonderful you are and that everyone is on your team to greatness. Every situation is for your good.

Let go the heavy baggage that keeps you stuck and weary. Forgive others, most importantly forgive yourself. We are all works in progress. Live joyfully rather than perfectly. Say "no gracias" (no thanks) to shame, suffering and fear. Let love reign. As I wrote in the *Preface* of the third edition of *Spirited Leadership: 52 Ways to Build Trust*:

What I considered punishment was simply preparation. We are always being prepared to do greater works. I now look at setbacks

as simply redirection and tweaking. There are no failures, simply feedback. We are meant for greatness.

My sincerest desire is to make your life easier, lighter and brighter by sharing the observations, insights and wisdom gained through rich experiences, both personally and professionally. Take the lessons with a giggle and a smile – I have enough gray hair for us all! And send me your questions or thoughts at GreaterYou@EllenCastro.com.

Your future is so bright you are going to need sunglasses!

> *Every sinner has a future and every saint has a past.*
>
> — DEEPAK CHOPRA

Introduction: Why a Parable?

> *It's not overly dramatic to say
> your destiny hangs upon
> the impression you make.*
>
> — BARBARA WALTERS

We live and work in a world where competence is no longer enough to succeed. According to Daniel Goleman, Ph.D., whose groundbreaking scholarly work literally defined the term, "emotional intelligence" accounts for up to 69% of job performance. *Happy in Spite of People* takes emotional intelligence from a scholarly approach to a practical, personally relevant and authentic approach to people and to life.

Being happy in spite of people is not a measure of higher education or an intelligence quotient. I have worked with genius-level college graduates with virtually no ability to connect with the myriad of personalities they meet every day. I have also watched the single mom waiting tables at my local diner who is comfortable, connected and successfully interacting with all personalities in the room.

We are all in the people business, regardless of where we are in life. No one is born with people genius, my term for emotional intelligence. But it is an essential skill and it can be learned. That's why I wrote this book – to be a guide to mastering better relationships, having more energy and achieving greater happiness and success in business and in life. As a globally-trusted coach and consultant to Fortune 500 companies, I believe that *genius, and greatness and greater success, flow through people and with people.*

Happy in Spite of People is a parable comprised of two sections. The first section, *"The Cats,"* provides relevant, real world proven techniques for identifying and thriving amid people's wide spectrum of personalities, including your own. The second section, *"Coaching in the Park,"* illustrates themes, reflections and insights to accelerate self-mastery and optimize the understanding of the human spirit and your interactions with others.

Why a parable? From my experience as a graduate student at both Harvard University and Southern Methodist University, business cases tend to be mental exercises only. Parables, on the other hand, have a life of their own. A parable is a simple story that illustrates a moral or a life lesson. Parables have been used throughout the ages and across cultures to illustrate truth and to provoke a response from the intellect *and* the heart. **Only when the heart is engaged can knowledge become wisdom.**

Parables have various layers of meaning. The level of understanding depends on the reader. Consider *The Wonderful Wizard of Oz*. Is it really just a fun story about a girl with red slippers, her dog and a wizard? Or, was Dorothy learning to trust her heart, to realize that no one could magically give her anything?

Happy in Spite of People has three layers. The first layer is entertainment. Reading through the stories provides a good laugh as you recognize the people in your life – and yourself – through the twelve complex personalities represented as cats with human personas.

The second layer teaches greater emotional intelligence, the people skills that will enable you to be a more energizing communicator, to build greater teamwork, to ignite passion and innovation, *and* to make you an invaluable asset to any business and to the community.

Dig a little deeper and you will find a third layer. Sit with the stories and reflect, and you will understand that *we are all multi-faceted*. Our behaviors create the perceptions that others have of us. **We are our choices.**

Our choices are driven by beliefs, conscious and unconscious, negative and positive. As you read through the parable, reflect on the beliefs that are driving your behaviors. The negative, self-defeating beliefs will keep you from your happiness, from your greatness and from your thriving. The positive beliefs are fuel for skyrocketing you to new levels of excellence, of self-expression, of improved people genius and of happiness. By consciously deciding to replace each negative belief with a powerful, positive belief, you will soar to new heights of success – in all its many forms.

Nothing changes out there until something changes within you. Happiness is a choice. Each of us has an inner voice. Consciously choosing to discover and to listen to that voice is your first step to liberating the genius and greatness within. Learning to trust that voice, and to trust that life is for you, are the crucial next steps to living *your* life boldly and fully – regardless of external factors. In doing so, you will be a happier, lighter and brighter conduit for inspiring and liberating the genius in others in your unique, extraordinary way.

Enjoy the journey! Dare to be a greater you!

*Pretend that every single person
you meet has a sign
around his or her neck that says,
'Make me feel important.'
Not only will you succeed in sales,
you will succeed in life.*

— Mary Kay Ash
Founder of Mary Kay Corp.
Her guiding principle: The Golden Rule.

*I praise you because
I am fearfully and wonderfully made.
Your works are wonderful,
I know that full well.*

— Psalms 139:14

Know Your Cats

Cat	Disposition	You ARE NOT this Personality? **To Thrive with this Personality:**	You ARE this Personality? **To Live Greater:**
Mr. P	• Catalyst • Collaborative	• Eliminate game playing • Accept and receive praise and constructive feedback • Enlist as a coach	• Sustain your healthier focus and choices • Spend more time listening to the genius within • Continue your attitude of gratefulness and celebrate your progress
Hoover	• Narcissistic • Self-absorbed	• Maintain your space and integrity • Expect this person to take credit • Resist temptation to compete for center stage	• Listen more and talk less • Stop all game playing • Allow others to be center stage
Peekaboo	• Timid • Fearful	• Ask for this person's thoughts and opinions • Exhibit common courtesy • Watch tonality and body language	• See yourself through the eyes of a loving God • Replace negative self-talk with positive, enriching self-talk • Listen to your heart, not your fears

Cat	Disposition	You ARE NOT this Personality? To Thrive with this Personality:	You ARE this Personality? To Live Greater:
Bondo	• Rescuer • "Do the Right Thing"	• Be reliable • Be appreciative • Avoid taking advantage	• Ask yourself, "Is this mine to do?" • Grasp the concept, "It's not all my fault." • Give yourself permission to live your gladness
Bruiser	• Dominating • Bullying	• Avoid or minimize exposure • Maintain position non-defensively • Ask yourself, "Would I rather be right or be happy?"	• Be aware of body language and tonality • Identify root cause of aggressive behavior • Imagine greatness by being respected instead of feared
Scarlett	• Dramatic • Reactive	• Model stability • Avoid being distracted • Remind yourself you cannot rescue this person	• Breathe through emotional swings • Get support • Take supplements or perhaps see a doctor
Willow	• Pleaser • Compromiser	• Be kind • Assist this person in building self-esteem • Provide feedback with diplomacy	• Say affirmations with kindness and self-love • Spend time enjoying your own company • Stop compromising your self-worth

Cat	Disposition	You ARE NOT this Personality? To Thrive with this Personality:	You ARE this Personality? To Live Greater:
Lucky	• Optimistic • Happy	• Be open to a new mindset • Enjoy the person's enthusiasm and positive energy • Ground his or her optimism with reality, only if appropriate	• Continue believing everything works together for good • Share your optimism and attitude of gratitude • Consider toning down your positive attitude based on audience and situation
Harvey	• Negative • Depressive	• Know it is not your job to change this person • Remain upbeat, positive • Be thankful you are more positive	• Forgive and release the past • Smile more and accept the encouragement you receive from others • Give yourself pats on the back
Luci	• Instigating • Manipulative	• Always go directly to the source to verify and to clarify information • Be 100% discerning and maintain your boundaries • Live your life in a way that others know the truth of who you are	• Stop all forms of lies and deceptions • Make right the wrongs • Choose kindness and service over jealousy and self-interest

Cat	Disposition	You ARE NOT this Personality? To Thrive with this Personality:	You ARE this Personality? To Live Greater:
Esperanza	• Harmonizing • Compassionate	• Allow and accept this person's grace-full presence • Recognize *your* actions determine whether this person is engaging or simply cordial • Relax and learn	• Share your light, learnings and love of life • Sow and water seeds of greatness in others • Find more avenues to share your light and to help others dare to be greater
Chen	• Sage • Wise	• Be honest and respectful • Gain from this person's insights and wisdom • Be thankful for a trusted mentor/ advisor	• Press on with your tireless focus to achieve more connection with God • Continue to be a conduit of healing by your presence, compassion and love • Share the living example of being happy, of genius and of success

The Cats

*We all live with the
objective of being happy;
our lives are different yet all the same.*

— Anne Frank

*You are far too smart to be the only thing
standing in your way.*

— Jennifer Freeman

*I've learned that people will
forget what you said,
people will forget what you did,
but people will never
forget how you made them feel.*

— Maya Angelou

Mr. P, The Cat-Alyst

Happy, relaxing and rejoicing, Mr. P was finally at peace in his own fur. Mr. P had made the colossal breakthrough from simply surviving to *thriving*. He understood he was purr-fect in his impurr-fections.

Mr. P, a twenty-one year young, black and white large-boned cat, was ecstatic that life was no longer a continual qualifying round. Life is to be enjoyed. Mr. P laughed out loud, "It took me nine lives, but who cares?

It's great to be me!

I am a marvel from head to paw!

Every moment is a gift!"

And with that, Mr. P danced his kitty samba. He was free from the constant anxiety of self-doubt and self-condemnation fed by the fears of rejection and abandonment. He had even lost his fear of being wrong. Mr. P knew he was part of a master plan. He was needed. He mattered. He was created on purr-pose, for a purr-pose.

The menacing dogs and the itchy fleas along with the catnip and the cat naps all worked together to create a truly meaningful life that Mr. P loved. Even though he occasionally fell out of a tree, he always landed on his big, white, fat paws.

"God loves me, fully and unconditionally!

Even though I've done some really dumb stuff,
I am still here and happy, too!"

Mr. P continued dancing. With his arms waving with gusto, Mr. P affirmed with joy,

"I love life and life loves me.

I am purr-riceless!

I am approved!"

Mr. P had finally realized there was nothing to figure out. He was supported and protected at all times. Mr. P could trust God, his Creator. It had been Mr. P's own thoughts, emotions and actions that had created most of the troubles, havoc, struggle and drama throughout his life. He wouldn't blame God.

Mr. P exuded a calm confidence, a deep knowing. Mr. P had finally accepted and received God's unfailing love. With faith, focus and discipline, Mr. P's self-defeating inner monologue had been exchanged for a life-enhancing dialogue with himself. Mr. P had learned to listen to the truth in his heart, the still, small voice within. He had found his sweet spot – to love himself and others to greatness.

Mr. P chuckled as he reflected that he still had a lot of listening to do. He was still here. Mr. P shared a stylish and whimsical home with his human mom. Their eclectic house was situated in a beautiful neighborhood with a lovely park that Mr. P graciously shared with the neighborhood dogs and squirrels.

Mr. P now understood that whether cats, dogs, squirrels, joggers, toddlers, moms or dads,

everyone was more alike than different.

He saw himself in everyone. It seemed every creature and human was searching for something. The "something" took many forms. Some called it happiness, and some called it approval or affection. Others called it credentials, wealth or power. Mr. P sensed that, whatever the name given, it all boiled down to a longing for acceptance, respect and love – *a sense of significance.*

Mr. P felt extremely fortunate for having found his "something." He was 97% living a life of happiness and pure delight. Mr. P hoped the remaining 3% would be without fleas and with a breeze. He had learned the secret for getting along with others and most importantly with himself.

Just love more.

The following stories are true. The names have been changed to protect the innocent, not so innocent and Mr. P.

Mr. P

You can trust Mr. Ps to be credible, compassionate, uplifting and collaborative.

If you are not a Mr. P, do this to thrive with Mr. Ps:

- Eliminate any and all game playing.
- Accept and receive their praise, positive reinforcement and uplifting, constructive feedback.
- Enlist them as your sounding board and coach.

Be open to the possibilities!

If you are a Mr. P, do this to soar to new heights of happiness:

- Sustain your faith and make better choices, including speaking only blessings.
- Spend more time listening to the genius within.
- Continue your attitude of gratitude and celebrate your progress.

Progress, not perfection.

Hoover, The Narcissist

Mr. P was in awe of the Creator's genius. As he was basking in the sun, he considered how his fur was thinner in the summer and noticeably thicker and warmer in the winter. All he had to do was groom himself. Mr. P marveled at the working of his heart. It pumped precious life-giving blood at 100,000 beats per day from head to paw. He was also inspired by the trees that inherently knew when to bud, to blossom and to grow.

It was at times like this when Mr. P was fully conscious; he knew that his path was prepared. All he had to do was the best with what he was given.

Everything was by design.

There were no wasted experiences.

Mr. P understood that trying to control what was not his to control with catfights and claws only led to frustration and suffering. Mr. P was thankful for his newfound thinking. There was no need to compete or to vie for attention since he was complete within. Mr. P had found that …

*The path to happiness
began by seeing yourself through
the eyes of a loving God.*

As Mr. P was enjoying the brilliant sunshine, Hoover waved enthusiastically to get his attention. Mr. P waved back at the silver cat and watched with amusement as Hoover worked the park. Hoover, while weight-challenged, considered his feline fat to be muscle. He adorned himself with his usual couture collar, this time his favorite Italian designer, Ar-meow-ni.

Hoover was a textbook case for narcissism. Narcissists are totally self-absorbed with an insatiable need for attention, adoration and control. They perceive themselves as the cat's pajamas, all knowing and absolutely purr-fect. Narcissists interfere with everyone and know no boundaries since they believe they know best *and* that the world revolves around them.

Hoover sauntered over and asked, "Hi, Mr. P, how are you today?"

"Hi, Hoover. I am so excited! I have a new water bowl!" Before Mr. P could utter another word, Hoover interjected, "I am sure it is very nice. You should see the water bowl I have! It's actually a fountain with a filter. Of course, it sits on a custom platform in my mansion …" The race was on. If a fellow feline had the flu, Hoover's bout and overnight veterinary stay was life-threatening.

While at first other cats would be enthralled with Hoover's charm, the feeling would quickly wear off. Prolonged exposure to Hoover made everybody like the "walking dead." He would suck the very life energy from his unsuspecting audience like the high-powered vacuum cleaner that Hoover bragged was named after him.

Yes, audience. Hoover was always on center stage. He was the perpetual silver-tongued spin master and game player. When Hoover gave, it was always with a motive. He played multiple roles and wore many masks to gain control at all costs. Hoover's demanding need was a result of his very early kittenhood.

Hoover recounted the sad details to all who would listen, yet he could never be truly vulnerable and would never let anyone really see who he was. He was afraid. Hoover held a deep, abiding fear that others would notice the gaping hole in his self-worth that he tried desperately to fill with stuff. Sadly, it was essential to Hoover's fragile ego that no one shined more brightly than he. It wasn't personal. He just *had* to be number one.

> Having to be number one
> was quite a heavy burden for him to carry
> and even a heavier burden for others to endure.

One day, Hoover would be a benevolent benefactor. The next day, he would be the menace. His role depended on whether you worshipped him, whether he could use you, or if he saw you as a threat. It was all a charade, a well-constructed house of cards. The problem with a house of cards is that it only takes one card to be removed for the whole house to collapse.

Mr. P let out a big sigh. Life could not be controlled.

Only one's own thoughts, emotions and actions can be controlled.

If those thoughts, emotions and actions created a foundation of trust and credibility, Mr. P knew life would always work out for the best. Mr. P hoped one day Hoover would know this powerful truth.

Hoover

You can trust Hoovers to be totally self-absorbed.

If you are not a Hoover, do this to thrive with the Hoovers:

- Maintain your space and integrity.
- Expect them to take credit for your successes.
- Resist the temptation to compete for center stage. It is a waste of energy!

Accept people for who they are.

If you have Hoover tendencies, do this to gain more social awareness and people skills:

- Listen more and talk less.
- Stop all game playing.
- Allow others, when appropriate, to be center stage regardless of your urge to be number one.
- Consider the concept that it is not how bright you shine, but how bright you help others shine.

Credit is for sharing.

Peekaboo, The Timid Cat

As Mr. P entered his luscious green blossoming garden, he saw a cat cowering beneath the statue of an angel. The angel's name was Faith.

Mr. P whispered, "Come out little cat. What is your name? My name is Mr. P." There was no movement. Again, Mr. P asked her name ever so gently, adding this time, "You are safe."

With this assurance, the cautious, timid cat slowly made her appearance. Mr. P's heart sank as he saw the fear in her anxious hazel eyes. There were patches of bare skin where her beautiful fur once was. He knew the massive clumps had fallen out due to stress and despair.

She meekly replied, "My name is Peekaboo."

Mr. P replied, "What a lovely name you have. It sounds so playful and reminds me of the game the human children play called 'hide and seek'."

She answered, "I wish my name was meant to be playful. I am named Peekaboo because I am afraid of everything. I only come out when no one is there."

Mr. P looked directly and compassionately into her eyes. Mr. P wanted her to know she was not alone in this world. "Tell me, Peekaboo, why are you afraid of everything?"

With barely an audible voice, Peekaboo answered, "Every time I am visible, something bad happens. I am told, 'Scat, you ugly cat!'"

"Peekaboo, you ugly? No way. You have lovely hazel eyes. It is obvious you are kind and have a good heart. That makes you beautiful in my eyes and in the eyes of our Creator!"

Mr. P saw a faint smile on her quivering lips. He proceeded, "As for not being wanted, what makes you think you are not wanted? If you were not wanted, you would not be here. The truth is that each and every one of us is created for a singular and specific purr-pose that complements the whole. You *are* meant to be here, plain and simple."

With these encouraging words, Mr. P could see a teardrop roll down Peekaboo's matted cheek before she began to sob. Mr. P approached Peekaboo carefully, not wanting to spook her. She allowed him to rest next to her side. He sensed her relief. Peekaboo drifted to sleep. When she awoke, Mr. P was still beside her.

"Good morning, Peekaboo. I must leave for now because my mom is probably looking for me. You can stay here and rest if you like.

Know that our Creator is always with you.

You are never rejected, never abandoned
and always loved."

Peekaboo looked at him with wishful eyes, as if she wanted to believe what he was saying. Mr. P had gained the wisdom to listen with all his faculties – his ears, eyes and heart. He had learned that understanding others came from hearing more than their spoken words.

"Peekaboo, it is true. We are *always* loved. Until we meet again, Peekaboo, please do me a favor." Peekaboo nodded in agreement. "When you are feeling afraid, connect with God's presence. It is *always* available. Affirm to yourself…

I am approved.

I am divine.

Everything else is a lie."

Peekaboo gazed at him in bewilderment, "Approved?"

"Yes, Peekaboo. You are approved and meant to shine brightly as only you can. Repeat the affirmation to yourself often and out loud.

Imagine the words being absolutely true and how you would feel resting in this knowledge and in this truth. In fact, feel yourself embraced by heavenly hugs." At which point Mr. P fell to the emerald green grass wrapping himself in a four paw hug. "The change in your self-talk will change your thoughts, changing your thoughts will change your beliefs and actions, and slowly but surely your beliefs and actions will change your life, too!

The acceptance, safety and love you always sought already exist within you."

Mr. P gave her a wink, sprang up to his paws and gave Peekaboo the hug of her life. He pranced off as he heard his mom calling.

"Sweet P, where are you? Mommy loves you." Mr. P giggled. He knew it was the beginning of another day in paradise.

Paradise was always just a thought away.

Every thought counts.

Peekaboo

You can trust Peekaboos to maintain a low profile.

If you know a few Peekaboos, do this:

- Bring them "out of hiding" by asking for their thoughts and opinions, and by providing a safe environment for them to express themselves.
- Show common courtesy. It is more important than ever.
- Watch your tonality and body language. Appearing condescending, mean or patronizing will make the Peekaboos retreat and become invisible due to perceived safety threats.

Be kind.

If Peekaboo reminds you of you, do this to liberate your greatness:

- Reflect, identify and list the possible underlying cause(s) for your fear(s).
- Consciously remember to see yourself through the eyes of a loving God on your journey to self-love and greatness.
- Replace all negative, self-criticizing and fear ridden self-talk with positive, self-correcting and enriching self-talk.

- Smile at yourself in the mirror while affirming, "I am approved! In fact, I *am* extraordinary!"
- Become more visible by listening to your heart, not your fears.

Enter every situation knowing you are approved.

Bondo, The Fixer

It was a muggy afternoon at the park. The heaviness of the humidity disappeared when Mr. P spotted Bondo. Joy always came to Mr. P's heart when he saw Bondo. If there ever was a problem, Bondo was sure to come to the rescue. Even before a problem existed, Bondo was on it. Thank goodness he had short blond fur, since it appeared he took little time for himself.

Mr. P understood what drove Bondo to be "Super Bondo." It was an overwhelming sense of responsibility instilled by his parents while he was a part of the litter. Bondo's parents had been quite a pair. His dad was addicted to massive quantities of catnip, his mom a purr-fect victim. The combination created lots of chaos and drama during his kittenhood. Unintentionally, his parents had imprinted on his psyche, "It's all your fault. Fix it." This applied to everything, from tidying up the home, to finding treats, to even controlling the weather.

Since birth, Bondo had desperately tried to calm his parents' high emotions by being the purr-fect cat. Mr. P had a lot of respect for Bondo. Instead of being a disaster like his siblings, Bondo had chosen to be a model cat-citizen. Today, the mugginess seemed to be weighing Bondo down as he lumbered slowly to Mr. P.

"Mr. P, how are you? I am so sorry about the weather being a bummer."

"I'm doing wonderfully, Bondo. I am quite sure you are not at fault for the weather, Bondo.

It is not always your fault.

How are you?"

"Actually, I'm worn out. I can't seem to shake the gloominess I am feeling. I know I should help others, but …," Bondo replied as he gazed off into the distance.

"Bondo, it is absolutely okay to not always help others. Adult cats need to help themselves.

You are *not* accountable for another's happiness.

A very wise human once said we were created to be accountable for ourselves and to be the change we want to see in this world."

Bondo returned his gaze to Mr. P with tired blue sunken eyes. "It really is a burden to feel responsible for everyone. How did you know?"

"Experience is a good teacher, Bondo. You never have to feel depleted again or live in desperation to please others. You do need to start taking care of yourself. Let others find their happiness. It is not your job. From what you told me about your kittenhood, you were the parent when it seemed that your parents were incapable of taking care of themselves."

Bondo let out a gigantic sigh. "Could it be that basic? How do I fix it?"

"Every time you feel the urge to rescue someone, ask yourself …

'Is this mine to do?'

There is a big difference between *wanting* to help others and *needing* to rescue them. Wise cats are accountable for their *own* actions and consequences and don't feel the need to fix everything for others. They accomplish more by being still and listening to their inner kitty. Their help is a form of true love. Rescuing is just a Band-Aid for those you are rescuing because it temporarily fixes the problem and a Band-Aid for you because it gives you a moment of self-worth because you rescued them."

Mr. P noticed that Bondo had begun to lick his bald stress patch. Mr. P had touched a nerve. "What are you thinking, Bondo?"

"Logically, it makes sense. Emotionally, it is a scary concept."

"It would be abnormal if it weren't scary, Bondo. Any new awareness takes time to process and to integrate into our way of thinking. Be patient. Give yourself time. Do you know what I believe? I believe your mere presence adds value. I believe you deserve a Medal of Valor for choosing to be a model cat-citizen in spite of your rough start in life. It is time for you to believe that you are awesome. It is time to feel to your core …

You are wonderfully made.

You can be anything you want to be."

Bondo was smiling, his blue eyes becoming brighter. He had stopped licking his stress patch.

Mr. P continued, "God wants us to live the joy He placed in our individual hearts, Bondo. I discovered we do not receive true joy from rescuing others. We do, however, help others and have lasting happiness by expressing the fullness of joy that is already within us. God wants us to live fully by shedding the limitations and labels imposed by our well-meaning parents and guardians.

God created you for a purr-pose that only you can fulfill.

You are custom designed."

Mr. P said with a broad smile and sparkling green irises, "Bondo, 'til we meet again, affirm to yourself …

I deserve my own self-care.

I am accountable for my happiness.

I will allow others to be accountable for theirs."

Bondo trotted off briskly with a newfound hope. Mr. P knew Bondo would commit to his affirmations because he was a conscientious cat. Mr. P would easily observe Bondo's progress by seeing his stress patch filling in.

Mr. P was now doing the kitty Macarena with his front white paws outstretched in a "Y" signaling "Yeah for me!"

Yeah to the joy and goodness of life!

Yeah because we are meant for greatness in this life!

Bondo

You can trust Bondos to do the right thing.

If you have Bondos in your life, do this with them to thrive:

- Be as reliable as they are.
- Be appreciative of their efforts.
- Avoid taking advantage of their good nature since you reap what you sow – eventually, always.

Be accountable for your own life and happiness.

If you tend to get "bald patches," do this to live your joy and expand your greatness:

- Ask yourself, *"Is this mine to do?"* when you feel the urgent need to fix it.
- Fully grasp the concept, "It's not all my fault."
- Give yourself permission to live your gladness and soar!

Wear your Medal of Valor with joy.

Bruiser, The Alpha Cat

Mr. P was having a glorious catnap under one of the many oak trees in his park. He was purr-fectly happy as he dreamed of big cloud fish in the sky. He was startled by a pushy paw nudging him awake.

"What? Bruiser, is everything okay? I was having the best dream." Bruiser was an alpha cat. While he was slight in body, Bruiser was built like a brick wall. Bruiser's de-mean-or tended toward the meaner side. His energy was oppressing; so were his looks. Bruiser had spiked hair, sharpened teeth and a thick leather collar with sharp pointed studs.

"Everything is certainly not okay, Mr. P! You know this is *my* favorite tree!"

Mr. P stretched out and opened his cat eyes more fully. "Is it? I thought it was *that* tree over there," as he pointed his furry paw to a different oak tree.

"You are wrong! It is *this* tree," responded Bruiser with a huff.

Bless Bruiser's heart. He could not get past his past.

In a moment of vulnerability, Bruiser had once shared that he had grown up in a tough neighborhood. He had been the runt of the litter, and to survive he had become aggressive. He had sworn he would never be bullied again. Bruiser's parents compounded his fighter's mentality by assuring him life was a struggle and a fight, so "get used to it!"

We get what we expect.

So even though Bruiser now lived on Easy Street, he recreated another tough environment.

"Oh, Bruiser, I am sure I saw you marking *that* tree with another cat." This time Mr. P's tail was pointing in the direction of the tree.

"Are you mocking me? You don't want me as your enemy, Mr. P." Bruiser said in a menacing manner.

"Bruiser, I don't want any enemies. I heard once and found it true that …

What you attack, you must fear.

I was just providing my observation." It was then Mr. P realized the accusing tone of his observation had carried a lot of judgment.

"I apologize, Bruiser. Perhaps I was trying to provoke you since you provoked me out of a purr-fectly sound nap. Please accept my apologies."

"I do not want your apologies or observations, Mr. P. I want you to leave this tree now. Or are you cruisin' for a bruisin'?" That was Bruiser's signature slogan.

"Bruiser, I am happy with whatever tree, for I am happy on the inside. I have nothing to prove." Mr. P began to strut away when he slowly began to regret he had not just changed trees from the start. "Oops!" Mr. P's ego was still alive and well.

Mr. P let out a sigh. He was thankful for the "oops factor." He had learned to stop beating himself up when he made a mistake, to stop his obsessive self-criticism. Instead Mr. P would say, "Oops," and then forgive himself and do better next time by responding, not emotionally reacting. Finally, he learned to accept that he was a cat, not a saint. "I forgive myself.

I am a work in progress."

"Don't you walk away from me, Mr. P. Are you implying I am not happy with myself? All creatures know me and fear me. I control the park." Bruiser was pounding his paws on his broad muscular chest as though he was king of the concrete jungle.

"Good for you, Bruiser, if that is what you want. Have a nice afternoon. Again, I apologize." Mr. P walked away slowly.

Mr. P had learned that you can't pick a fight with someone who refuses to participate. There were so many things Mr. P wanted to blurt out including …

Actions have consequences.

There is always a payback.

You are the one making your life hard.

But he knew this was not the time for these comments to be said out loud. While they might be valid, Mr. P knew the moment was emotionally charged.

Mr. P wanted to make sure he was coming from his healthy ego before he commented further. Mr. P's intent in the previous moment was to be right at all costs – including at the cost of Bruiser – to show Bruiser that he was superior and enlightened. Mr. P chuckled to himself. This was a sure sign of a super ego, *not* enlightenment.

Mr. P knew there was always fallout, sooner or later, with the super-sized ego. Just as super-sized fries at the drive-thru are not good for the body, super-sized egos are not good for the spirit. They are also detrimental for creating relationships built on trust and happiness.

Mr. P grinned, knowing he would be given several more opportunities to get it right. Life had a sense of humor.

Bruiser

You can trust Bruisers to use intimidation.

If you encounter Bruisers, do this to thrive with them:

- Avoid them if possible or minimize your exposure.
- Maintain your position non-defensively.
- Ask yourself, "Would I rather be right or be happy?"

Learn to choose your battles.

If you are sometimes a Bruiser, do this so you can skyrocket to greater success:

- Become more aware of your body language and tonality.
- Identify what is driving your aggressive behaviors. List how many more resources you have today compared to when the cause of the bully-like behavior was instilled as a sense of survival.
- Consider affirming, *"The past has lost its power over me."*
- Imagine you were respected by others instead of feared. List three positive outcomes and three actions that would support the shift to being respected.

Life is for you.

Scarlett, The Drama Queen

Seeing Scarlett always put Mr. P in a profound state of gratitude.

"Thank you, God!

I am free from the past and its craziness.

I am here and happy.

The rest of my life is the best of my life!"

Prior to this knowingness, Mr. P had been *the* drama king. His life had been a series of ups and downs; *everything* triggered an intense emotion and reaction, just like it now did for Scarlett. This particular day, Scarlett was in rare form even for her.

Scarlett was like the biggest roller coaster ride at a theme park – the highest highs and the lowest lows. Life was either oh-so-wonderful or oh-so-cat-astrophic. There was no middle ground. You could easily identify Scarlett's mood by her body language.

When life was intensely wonderful, Scarlett's long red fur was shiny and groomed. Her hips would confidently sway as her strut captured every cat's attention. When life would take its inevitable dips, so did her hips. They would fall low to the ground and almost drag. Even her purr-fect fur lost its luster.

Today was an obvious down day. "Oh, Mr. P, I feel awful. The worst thing has happened. I broke a nail! Today of all days with a birthday party to go to. What shall I do?" She thrust her broken nail in his face.

Mr. P was about to laugh and then reconsidered since this would have been a big deal to him once upon a time. He knew and understood how fragile one could be with the dizzying effects of the perpetual turns, twists, ups and downs of what seemed an endless ride.

"Oh, Scarlett, go and have fun. You were invited for you, not your nails. Plus the attention will be on the birthday cat."

"You are right, Mr. P, the attention should be on her. Why can't I be more like you? You seem to take life as it comes. Are you on medication?"

Mr. P could not contain his laughter. "Thank you, Scarlett. What a fantastic compliment. I used to be on medication. My life was a roller coaster ride with the mood swings to match," he chuckled. "I guess my human mom was worried and probably exhausted from my emotional cat swings herself; so she took me to see Deborah, the cat whisperer."

"A cat whisperer?"

"Yes, a vet for the soul. All it took was about a minute. I was on medication. I felt like a *total* loser." Scarlett stared at him with piercing racing eyes as though Mr. P had touched a nerve.

Mr. P continued, "It was as though Deborah was reading my mind. She petted me and said, 'God loves us so much. He created medication to help us through life when needed. Just like insulin for our friends who have diabetes and nitroglycerine for our friends who have heart problems. It is purr-fectly okay to have help with your brain chemistry balance.'"

Scarlett had settled next to Mr. P. "Please tell me more."

"You'll be late for your party if I do."

Scarlett sprang up, hips once again in full swing, and called back, "Oh, how I do love parties. Tomorrow is another day."

With that, Mr. P smiled and waved back, and saying to himself, "Tomorrow *is* another day. Isn't it wonderful …

Each day starts fresh with new mercy and grace.

Each day presents an opportunity for a new beginning."

Scarlett

You can trust Scarletts to make life exciting.

If some Scarletts enter your scene, do this to thrive with them:

- Model stability and be an anchor.
- Avoid being distracted from what is yours to do.
- Remind yourself you cannot rescue them; they must save themselves.

Stay centered.

If your life feels like a theme park roller coaster ride, do this to live from the stability and greatness within:

- Observe emotional swings. While breathing through the emotions and feelings, affirm calmly to yourself, "The world did not stop with this."
- Know that emotions and feelings will pass. They are just messages and patterns surfacing for you to gain fresh insight, more understanding and the wisdom to change.
- Get support. Join a faith-based group or other associations that resonate with your heart. Professionals are invaluable, too, in discovering the underlying beliefs driving the mood swings and your unconscious need for drama.

- Take supplements or perhaps see a doctor. There is no shame or stigma to being on medication or seeking help except in your own mind.

You are not your emotions.

Willow, The Pleaser

Mr. P was happily doing his daily "yoga paws" in the park. He delighted in stretching his body for the good of his health. The movements connected him to the purr-fect moment – *now*. In the *now* there was freedom from the past and a fresh future.

In the now there was love.

Even though Mr. P sensed he was being watched, he continued with his sun salutation. Stretch, bend backwards, lunge. He felt he might be setting a good example, plus he was having fun.

One always needed to take time for fun.

Upon completing his pose, Mr. P opened his eyes and gently gazed at Willow. Willow was a beautiful cat in all ways. She had shining dark brown fur and big brown eyes; Willow, however, could not see her beauty. As her name implied, Willow would bend and sway at the whims of others. She was the ultimate pleaser, often at her own expense. While being adaptable was a good quality, it was not good when it compromised Willow's sense of personal identity and self-worth.

Willow wore her heart out on her paw, willing to give it away for the least bit of attention or the tiniest speck of love. Mr. P, the purr-fect cat-alyst for change, realized that the root of all fearful behavior, from obsessive controlling to continually giving one's self away, was rooted in kittenhood.

> Regardless of the best, most loving parents and caretakers, no cat left kittenhood unscathed.

Willow's overwhelming, endless need for love and attention was instilled and cemented in her youth. Willow's birth mother had been so unstable she had taken her life in a moment of despair. Her "good" parent, her dad, was self-absorbed and inattentive. Though he was an extremely successful cat, he felt cheated when any creature was more fortunate than he. None of his successes were ever enough because he could not comprehend that he was already enough.

Poor Willow was not enough for him either. She had gnawed through cement to no avail trying to gain any sign of approval and love. Unintentionally, yet just the same, the patterns of self-hatred of both parents were passed on to her.

Mr. P nuzzled Willow with a wet, cold nose and asked, "Hi, Willow, how are you?"

Her big brown eyes were desperately seeking approval. She couldn't speak, or the tears would flow. Willow found her voice and purred, "Mr.

P, are you my Prince Charming, here to rescue me? Has my fairy tale come true?"

"Please do not get me started about fairy tales, Willow. They have created a lot of illusions and false expectations. You don't need a prince to come and to rescue you. There is a 'happily ever after' for you, Willow. It has been trapped within you under the years of broken promises and not knowing the truth of who you are.

> You are purr-riceless and purr-fect,
> lovable and loved.
>
> You are divine!"

Mr. P proceeded compassionately, "Willow, I admit you did have a tragic start. You did not deserve it, yet it was the hand you were dealt. It is how you choose to play the deck that counts.

> *People and the past only have the power you give them.*

Trust me, Willow, experts can be wrong.

> *Your gene pool, past or environment do not define you.*
>
> *You define you by your choices.*
>
> *Every choice counts.*

You are far more powerful than you imagine. Now is your moment of power. The approval you are seeking lies within you. Got it?!!"

Willow was startled yet inspired by Mr. P's directness today. "Got it, Mr. P."

"Willow, I am going to give you a statement I want you to repeat to yourself with conviction over and over again, until it sinks in.

To know me is to love me.

Worthy, that's me!"

"Ha-ha-ha, you do have a sense of humor, Mr. P," replied Willow.

"This is not a laughing matter, Willow. Do you want to stop being an approval junkie?"

"Yes, I do. You make me sound like a drug addict."

"You are an addict. You are addicted to the high you get when someone approves of you. For every high, Willow, there is always a corresponding low. It is a natural law. You know that, you've been there."

"Yes, I have, Mr. P. I promise to begin repeating …

To know me is to love me.

Worthy, that's me!"

A heavy weight fell off of Willow's shoulders. Her heart was healing and opening with those words. Willow bounced home, lighter and happier.

Mr. P beamed. Life is great. Dreams do come true. He was living "happily ever after."

Willow

You can trust Willows to wear their heart on their sleeve.

To thrive with the Willows, do this:

- Be kind.
- Assist them in building their self-esteem by articulating their gifts, their strengths and positive qualities.
- Provide constructive feedback with diplomacy.

Provide reassuring smiles.

If you are a Willow searching for approval at all costs, do this to skyrocket to self-love and to greatness:

- Say your affirmations with the kindness, love and approval you always wanted to hear.
- Let the truth sink in – *you are priceless, precious and lovable to the core.*
- Remember *experts can be wrong.*
- Begin spending time enjoying and celebrating your own company.
- Laugh the next time you are about to compromise your self-worth and say, "Not this time. Worthy, that's me!"

The love and approval you seek is already within you waiting to be discovered.

Lucky, The Happy Cat

Today at the park, Mr. P was once again reminded of the power that thoughts have. If you want your life to change, you have to change the way you think.

Mr. P knew from his personal experience that bad attitudes and destructive behaviors could be changed when you changed your thinking. When you changed from self-defeating thoughts to life-affirming thoughts, your reality improved. When your reality improved, your beliefs changed. Your world changed for the better.

Mr. P had consciously chosen to change his cycle of surviving and suffering to one of trust and thriving by assuming that life was for him. In reality, everything happened for him, not to him.

Life was altogether good.

This single shift in belief was one of the best choices Mr. P felt he had ever made.

Lucky, the happy cat, always made Mr. P's whiskers wiggle with bliss because Lucky was the purr-fect reminder of choosing life-affirming perspectives and attitudes. Lucky was an average-sized striped cat. He had the bubbliest disposition. Lucky had one leg that was a brownish-yellow, one leg orange and another leg white. Yep, Lucky had three legs.

It was an inspiration to see Lucky hop along with the biggest smile and the greatest of ease while waving at his friends – although this often made him stumble – and stopping to introduce himself to any newcomers. The newcomers included cats, dogs, birds, squirrels and humans – everyone! Lucky was never threatened or intimidated, just here and happy.

"What's your name? I'm Lucky."

Mr. P never tired of hearing the conversation that always ensued. "Lucky? How can that be, you only have three legs?"

"My name *is* Lucky. And yes, I *am* lucky! I still have three good legs left."

Lucky was loved by the 99% who were invigorated by his joy of living. There was that 1% who were annoyed and would try to dampen his spirit. Lucky did not care. He would just smile and literally "shake it off," which made for an interesting, sometimes comical and even more inspirational sight to behold.

Mr. P had no clue as to whether Lucky had been born with the gift of optimism by viewing obstacles as opportunities or if he had learned to have a positive attitude. What mattered was that he got it.

Lucky was, in fact, a very lucky cat.

Lucky

You can trust Luckys to have a positive outlook and find the good in every situation.

If you are lucky enough to have Luckys in your life, do this to thrive with them:

- Be open to allowing and receiving a new mindset.
- Enjoy their enthusiasm and positive energy.
- Ground their optimism in reality *only* when appropriate and in *their* best interest.

Think "Yes!"

If you are lucky enough to be a Lucky, do this to continue to enjoy the good life:

- Continue your belief that everything works together for good.
- Share your contagious optimism and attitude of gratitude.
- Consider toning down your positive attitude to be taken more seriously – less of a Pollyanna – based on the audience and situation.

Stay happy and optimistic in spite of people.

9

Harvey, The Wounded Cat

As much as Mr. P was thrilled to see Lucky, Mr. P's heart sank when watching Harvey.

Harvey was the polar opposite of Lucky. Harvey was a handsome, athletic, midnight-blue cat. Although he had four strong legs and no apparent physical challenges, Harvey was emotionally handicapped. He saw his water bowl half-empty instead of half-full. Harvey had a downer disposition. "Why me?" was his mopey meow. Regardless of how others tried to encourage him with cat tales of how wonderful he or his life was, Harvey enjoyed wallowing in self-pity and misery. Mr. P tried to cheer Harvey up.

"Good afternoon, Harvey. What a great day! You look well." Mr. P offered as he looked upon Harvey's sad countenance.

Harvey rolled his eyes and said, "A great day? It is just another day. When will you learn to call me 'Nubs'? I told you, I've been declawed."

As Mr. P saw it, that was the root cause of his depressing disposition. "Harvey, I'd prefer calling you by your given name. That really is a bummer of a label you've given yourself."

"Fine, have it you way, Mr. P," Harvey replied sullenly and added, "I did not label myself. My owners did. You could never understand how I feel."

"Harvey, I have been declawed, too." Harvey stared in disbelief as Mr. P held up his two front paws and showed the empty pads.

"You and I are so much more than our claws. We must understand that our claws or lack of claws do not determine our worth or our identity." Harvey was still listening.

"Deborah, the cat whisperer, helped me get past the trauma and bitterness of losing my claws. She suggested different ways of looking at being declawed. For one, I am sure my human mother had no clue about the harm she was inflicting. She was treating me the way others taught her to treat cats. When I realized she had not harmed me maliciously, I began to forgive her. I say 'began' because …

Forgiveness is a process.

Harvey, here's how I moved on. Every time I think of the pain she caused me, I forgive her. Even if it's several times a day and years after it happened. Each time I become stronger and freer."

Harvey was confused and said so. "I don't get it, Mr. P. Forgiving her freed you? Those who have declawed me should be held responsible for what they did. They took away my claws, my self-respect."

"Yes, Harvey, they took away your claws, but as for your self-respect …

>No one can take away your self-respect;
>you give it away or you lose it by your actions.

It's time to regain your self-respect, Harvey. It's time to forgive. Unforgiveness is like a water bowl full of poison. You lap it up, thinking it will hurt the one who hurt you; but it ends up harming you, and sometimes it ruins your chance of future happiness and blessings. Forgive your owners, Harvey; stop the pity party and live."

Harvey's cat eyes were full of cat tears as his emotions began to soften from the years of hardening the shell of protection around his wounded heart.

Mr. P continued, "It has taken me a while, but now I see the gifts from being declawed. Harvey, hasn't being declawed made you more creative and resourceful? Haven't you learned other ways to defend yourself and escape harm? You haven't inadvertently clawed yourself either, have you? The greatest benefit to me is that it made me more alert and aware of my surroundings, more present and in the now. That is a very good thing."

Harvey could no longer keep the puddles of tears from streaming down his sapphire fur to his white whiskers. The healing had begun. Forgiveness found a way. Harvey felt a sprout of hope pushing through the broken shell around his heart. He smiled.

As they began their stroll through the richly scented grass, Mr. P asked, "Do you still insist on me calling you 'Nubs'?"

"My name is Harvey. Please call me Harvey."

Harvey

You can trust the Harveys to be negative and have a depressive presence.

If you are brought down by Harveys, do this to thrive with them:

- Remember it is not your job to rescue or change them – to encourage and to uplift, yes.
- Remain upbeat and positive.
- Give praise that you are more positive.

Happiness is a choice.

If you sometimes feel like you're Harvey, do this to unleash your greatness:

- Forgive the "who" and "what" of your past – rehashing and dwelling on the details of the past keeps you stuck in the past and poisons your future.
- Understand that to forgive does not mean you approve of what happened. It does mean you are willing and ready to leave the past behind you to live your best life now. If you can't seem to get past the past, ask yourself, "What is the payoff for staying angry?" *Is the perceived payoff really worth being stuck?*

- Smile more and stir up your unique gifts and talents by accepting the encouragement and compliments you receive from others.
- Give yourself pats on the back for making progress.

Learn to forgive instantly.

Luci, The Instigator

Mr. P was thoroughly enjoying another day in his park. While the weather itself was dreary, he felt happy. Mr. P had found the quickest routes to being here and happy were …

Being grateful.

Consciously connecting with God's presence.

Mr. P was grateful for all of his experiences that had eventually worked together for his good. Throughout his nine lives, every good and bad situation brought him to the place where he was today. He no longer felt the need to perform, to fight, to struggle or to create drama. He knew in his heart that …

God was the source of *all* supply.

The Creator wanted him to live life fully and abundantly.

God could be trusted.

"How glorious and exciting! I am safe, loved and protected. My God desires all cats to live a life of joy, prosperity and contentment."

Mr. P let out a freeing sigh. "Ahhhhhhh." It was then he noticed, out of the corner of his eye, his last remaining nemesis, Luci.

Mr. P could feel his heart pounding as old patterns and emotions of fear and dread swept him back to the past. Luci and Mr. P came from the same litter. They had the same mother and father, but they couldn't be more different from each other. Mr. P began to breathe more consciously – to come back to the present moment and regain his connection with God.

Luci was the blackest of black cats with cold, soulless eyes. While her name seemed cute, Mr. P was sure it was short for Lucifer. Luci embodied walking evil. She always left a path of darkness and destruction with her devious ways. Even her own kittens had not been spared.

Luci always played the victim. She would recount the details of the cruelty of her kittenhood, exaggerating the sadness and pain she faced each day. Luci played the "blame game." She easily sucked others into her wicked web constructed of half-truths, lies and deception. Her plot was to plant seeds of doubts about others, creating distrust and division. Divide and conquer was her modus operandi.

After years of being separated from her daily drama, Mr. P could observe her more objectively, even compassionately. He felt sadness for her and for her next victim. If only he could warn them. Unfortunately, she was too good at her role as a victim. Was sibling rivalry rearing its ugly head? No. It was truth as Mr. P saw it.

Not long ago, Mr. P had made a conscious decision not to have any contact with Luci. It was simpler and necessary for his sanity and for his continued well-being. Mr. P let go of the need to return evil with evil in the name of justice. He knew that one day Luci would reap what she had sown. It was a spiritual law as real as the law of gravity.

As Luci began her approach to Mr. P, he *consciously* chose to go in the direction of Lucky to help him practice his pole vaulting. As he moved towards Lucky,

Mr. P released Luci with forgiveness and a prayer,
and freed himself.

Luci

You can trust Lucis to create angst by their innuendos and manipulation.

If a Luci comes into your life, do this to thrive with them:

- Always go directly to the source to clarify and to verify all information.
- Be 100% discerning.
- Maintain your boundaries.
- Live your life in a way that builds a stellar reputation so that, regardless of innuendos, others know the truth of who you are.

Engaging is a choice.

If you have Luci tendencies, do this to allow for greatness:

- Stop all forms of lies, deception and manipulation.
- Make right the wrongs you have inflicted on others, if possible.
- Don't be shocked if people are weary of your actions, do the right thing anyway.
- Choose kindness and service towards others instead of jealousy and self-interest.

Learn to love.

Esperanza, The Harmonizer

Esperanza was an extraordinary cat. Even on a day like today with overcast skies and a forecast of thunderstorms, she shined. Her luminous white fur reflected light and made her glow like a feline angel. She was the purr-fect expression of poise and grace. While Esperanza was a mature cat, she approached life as a newborn kitten. Appropriately, Esperanza had been affectionately christened with the nickname "Sunshine."

Esperanza had an innocent heart that harbored no ill feelings toward any creature. Esperanza never appeared to be driven by any motive other than respect and love. Esperanza was kind.

Kindness is its own reward.

Esperanza was here, happy and thriving – relaxed in her own gorgeous, snow-white fur.

Mr. P was admiring Esperanza from afar. He instantaneously became anxious when Luci approached Esperanza. As Mr. P observed their interaction, he sensed that Esperanza remained content and somehow self-contained. He breathed slowly and deeply, sending Esperanza good energy. Having sensed the positive energy, Esperanza turned and smiled at Mr. P. She said her farewell to Luci and floated towards Mr. P.

"Hi, sweet P, I've missed you! How are you?"

"Always good, even better now, Sunshine," he beamed. "You look more relaxed than ever. What is your secret?"

She winked and replied,

"I'm glad to be me.

I trust life to be altogether good.

I trust God."

Esperanza then proceeded to nuzzle Mr. P's precious plump cheek with her wet petite nose.

Mr. P's eyes twinkled. Her mere presence brought him peace. "I like the sound of that, Esperanza. Help me understand how you maintain being content while engaging with Luci? Don't you know that Luci's coat is so shiny because she siphons out the joy and energy of other cats?"

"P, you are so funny! It is probably easier for me since she and I are not from the same litter. Family history can change the dynamics for sure. *We all need to be aware of the family drama we sometimes drag into other relationships.* I've only experienced Luci in small doses. To answer your question, I am cordial with Luci, but I do not engage with her. From my vantage point, I feel sad for Luci. She must be aware at some level that ...

> What you attack becomes a payback.

I wish that Luci would l-i-v-e, the exact opposite of e-v-i-l. An evil existence is not truly living. Darkness like that is a waste of precious energy, time and power."

Mr. P marveled at Esperanza's wisdom. "Wow, Esperanza, there is a difference between acting cordially and being engaging. Thanks! It seems like I am always learning."

"So am I, Mr. P. That is what makes life marvelously grand. We can keep learning until we get it right.

> *There is no failure, no shame –*
> *just learning and growing."*

Mr. P's heart fluttered because her words resonated within him. Esperanza went on to say, "Mr. P, I am so proud of you. You rock!"

Tears welled up in Mr. P's sparkling green cat eyes. "Oh, Esperanza, thank you." Mr. P did his happy dance by prancing on his massive tippy toes while joyfully swirling and shrilling with glee, "Woo-hoo! Yes! It is time to celebrate how far I have come.

Worthy, that's me!

There are no wasted experiences.

It's all purr-fect by design."

Esperanza

You can trust Esperanzas to energize and to create harmony and goodwill.

If you encounter Esperanzas, do this to thrive with them:

- Allow and accept their graceful presence.
- Recognize that *your* actions determine whether the Esperanzas engage with you and spur you on to greatness or whether they are simply cordial.
- Relax and learn.

Joyfully indulge in the good energy.

Thank goodness for the Esperanzas! If you happen to have this disposition, do this to continue uplifting others:

- Share your light, learnings, wisdom and love of life.
- Sow and water seeds of greatness in others.
- Find more avenues to share your light and help others dare to be greater.

Spread the love.

Chen, The Trusted Advisor

It was a stupendous Sunday in the park. Birds were chirping, squirrels were munching, bees were buzzing and buds were blooming. Mr. P was absorbing the radiant beauty of the moment and thrilled that it was all happening without his help or supervision.

The musical notes and sounds of nature singing, the collage of creation's colors and the sumptuous scents carried powerful messages for Mr. P.

"God is in the details.

All of God's creation has beauty, so do I.

If flowers can bloom, so can I.

If bees can fly, so can I.

I can let go now and relax. I can trust my life will unfold brilliantly, naturally. My path is prepared."

Mr. P felt tranquil. Heaven on earth is possible. Mr. P breathed deeply and affirmed to himself, "Peace, trust, light." A warm loving feeling overtook him as he thought of his beloved mentor and trusted advisor, Chen. Chen was an amazing chocolate brown cat from a neighborhood out East. Mr. P was delighted their paws had crossed. As the saying goes, when the student is ready, the teacher appears.

Chen exuded heavenly qualities grounded in earthly reality. Chen had a heart full of compassion for all creatures, small and large, rich and poor. Chen had mastered the balance of being selfless while not losing one's self. His kindness and generosity were gifts of the Spirit. The touch of his paws brought comfort and healing to body, mind, spirit and soul.

Chen had the uncanny abilities to deflect any harm that was directed his way and to avoid being sucked into the hysterics, drama and demands of other cats. Mr. P asked on more than a few occasions, "How do you do it, Chen? I try and try but cannot master your technique of always being unaffected by the negativity and unrealistic expectations of others."

Chen's reply was always the same. "Mr. P, it is quite simple," as he wrinkled his nose …

"It is their dirty litter, not mine."

Mr. P's response was always the same, purring while stifling a giggle.

Chen continued as he leaned back and placed a paw over his belly, "God is my source. He is my source of strength, my source of direction and my source of peace.

*When I stay connected to my source,
life flows freely and gracefully.*"

"Oh, Chen, if only I could maintain my focus and composure 100% of the time like you."

"P, you will. Simply focus on the connection. Practice. You will always be given the opportunity to practice.

That is life – to learn, to grow, to trust."

With that memory fresh in his mind, Mr. P heard the melodies of nature more profoundly. The colors seemed more vivid, the flowers more fragrant. Mr. P had a deep respect for Chen and wanted to be more like him. Chen never imposed his will.

He simply lived his message.

"Peace, trust, light, huh?" Mr. P thought to himself while he heard the rumblings of a cat fight. "Guess it is time to practice." Mr. P turned his head with curiosity and saw what the commotion was. Hoover and Bruiser were fighting. They each had, Mr. P knew, something to prove.

All of a sudden, Mr. P caught a whiff of their dirty litter. "Peow-wie!" Practice makes purr-fect.

Chen

You can trust Chens.

If you run into some Chens, do this to thrive with them:

- Be honest and respectful.
- Be open to gain from their insights and wisdom.
- Be thankful for a trusted mentor and advisor.

Be a student and life-long learner.

If you are a Chen, do this to continue making the galaxy brighter and greater:

- Press on with your tireless focus to achieve more connection with God.
- Continue to comfort and to heal others by your presence, by your compassion and by your love.
- Share the living example of being happy, of greatness and of success in all its many forms.

Keep living your life as a sermon and inspiration.

Coaching in the Park

The most important single ingredient in the formula for success is knowing how to get along with people.

— THEODORE ROOSEVELT

If you're rubbed by every rub, how will you be polished?

— RUMI

If life is a game, aren't we all on the same team?

— KID PRESIDENT

Clash of the Egos

Affirming "peace, trust, light," Mr. P approached the boisterous sounds and stinky smell of dirty litter. A crowd was gathering, which was unfortunate since egos love an audience to display their cleverness and self-perceived power. It was the nature of the Bruisers and Hoovers to win at the cost of others, to keep score and to refuse to ask for help. For them, asking for help was a sign of weakness instead of a sign of strength that it is.

Mr. P knew that meaningful success is when everyone wins. Win/win was not in Bruiser's and Hoover's vocabulary; neither was listening. They loved the sound of their own voices almost as much as winning. Even when they appeared to be listening to others, they were either contemplating their response or gathering ammunition to further their position.

Mr. P had to grin, knowing that he too had loved the sound of his voice. He was grateful he had conquered the overpowering impulses to be right at all costs and the need to change others to the right way of thinking – his way of thinking.

"Whew, it really is difficult to learn and to grow
when you are always talking and defending your old, tired beliefs."

Of course, the change had taken thousands of swats to Mr. P's ego to grasp that it was *he* who needed to change, not others. His role was to inspire and perhaps to motivate others to change by role modeling good intentions *and* good actions. To actually change others was out of his sphere of control and responsibility.

Mr. P reflected that change had usually occurred for him for three reasons. One, the pain was too great not to change. Two, the gain was so wonderful it was worth the effort. Three, Mr. P had an epiphany, a paradigm shifting from an old way of thinking that inspired and instilled a change in beliefs and actions. While Mr. P liked the epiphanies, they were often associated with pain; so he was now opting for the gain payoff. Smart cat.

Mr. P was now in range to hear the heated debate.

"You are not listening, Hoover. The sky is obviously turquoise blue, like the ocean in Cat-cun with scattered clouds," Bruiser said. Bruiser was now sporting the fresh ink of a cat-too on the shaved bulging muscle of his foreleg.

"It is you, my friend, who is not hearing me. It is a cloudy day and the sky is bluish-green," Hoover replied as he invaded Bruiser's space. Mr. P's furry butt cheeks clenched as he heard "friend" spoken in such an unfriendly way.

"Oh, Hoover, your blue eyes must be color blind. There is nothing green about that sky." Bruiser was now using a patronizing tone to match Hoover's intimidating stance.

"So this is what the fireworks are about?" Mr. P threw his white fat paw over his mouth to keep from laughing out loud. What a waste of precious energy.

Many of the feline audience were holding their breath as the volume grew louder and the intensity magnified. The crowd was turning into a bunch of nervous scare-dy cats. Mr. P knew what he had to do. He began to consciously breathe slowly, calmly, deeply while repeating to himself, "Peace, trust, light." Even though the debate escalated, the anxiety began to lift as the other cats began to unconsciously breathe in unison with Mr. P's breathing. As the energy shifted, the eyes of the squirrels, birds, cats and dogs first met in puzzlement and then they all smiled. Some chuckled.

Mr. P overhead one of the comments …

"Fascinating, the more they try to appear big,
the smaller they actually become."

Bruiser and Hoover were so focused on their ego contest they failed to notice that the crowd had dispersed. When they did finally notice, Hoover and Bruiser decided to call it a truce since there were no remaining onlookers. Mr. P's work was done.

"Peace, trust, light." It worked! As Mr. P consciously expanded his love, fear lifted.

Coaching Moments

You can trust the bigger the ego, the bigger the eventual fall.

To thrive with others and in life, know and understand that *actions always have consequences.* You reap what your sow; there are no neutral actions.

Try this to skyrocket to greater success *with* others:

- Ask yourself these questions:

    "Does having the last word and having to always be right foster trust, lively discussions, collaboration and innovation?"

    "Am I giving away my credibility and long term effectiveness for the short term perceived gain?"

    "Will I or my organization stay relevant and competitive if we are not open to new ideas or willing to seek help, to change or to learn?"

- Identify what is driving your *need* to be right at all costs. Please be willing to dive deeper to understand what beliefs could be keeping you from your true greatness and more happiness.

Describe the worst case scenario if you replied, "Thank you for the new perspective. Tell me more."

As a point of reference, when I began my executive coaching practice, I felt I *had* to have all the answers. I did not want to appear stupid. As I gained more self-confidence, I realized I did not have to have all the answers – no one does. You can, however, ask the right questions that spark conversations and ignite innovation and results.

- Identify three behaviors and actions you can start implementing today to create a climate of win/win, excellence, innovation and synergy to soar to new heights.

Redefine power to be a greater you.

Unwound and Unlimited

Daybreak at the park was exhilarating to Mr. P. The vibrant yellow daffodils resembled miniature suns. The sound of the sprinklers' synchronized dance of water as it soaked the thirsty baseball field was beautiful and energizing. Watching the playful squirrels in the bleachers was entertaining. Mr. P purred slowly to squelch his urge to pounce on the squirrels. "Today will be a great day!"

> Every day was a great day when
> Mr. P stepped into the presence of his Creator
> and remained there.

Mr. P was grateful to have learned the above secret to living "happily ever after."

> There was no falling out of grace with God.

> It was Mr. P's choice to connect and to receive it.

If there was ever a time for the kitty cha-cha, it was now. The curse was broken. He was no longer held prisoner by his past, nor held hostage by labels and self-imposed limitations. His thoughts of fear and self-doubt were gone, the anxious knots unraveled. Mr. P was unwound and unlimited.

"To know me is to love me.

I am lovable and loved.

I am enough!"

Mr. P was not the least bit embarrassed by his cha-cha-cha celebration, even when he noticed Willow's gaze fixated on him.

"Come join me, Willow!" That was all the encouragement Willow needed. She pounced on Mr. P with such a force they both tumbled to the earth. As they rolled about, they meowed with the innocence and excitement of kittens. "Willow, I can't breathe. I am a senior citizen, you know."

Willow responded, "Mr. P, there is nothing senior about you!"

Mr. P grinned from pointed ear to pointed ear, "Have you been doing your homework?"

"Absolutely! The affirmations are making a positive and exciting difference. I am discovering my own self-worth. I don't feel nearly as lonely. I'm actually discovering several things that I like about myself. I am resilient. I am a smart cat to have survived the traumas of my kittenhood. I do have a big heart, and I am good-natured. I came to the wonderful realization that somebody does love me."

"Who would that be, besides me?" cha-cha-cha-ed Mr. P.

Willow giggled. "Besides you, Mr. P, God must totally love me. I'm here and smiling more."

"Willow, you are definitely on the right track. Your self-worth will increase as you recognize all the good, the gifts and the talents that reside within you. Finding the good and the true you is a journey. There will be speed bumps along the way, just like those around the park. Be patient and gentle with yourself as you move through the process of gaining more self-respect and self-love."

"Mr. P, why are you always so kind to me?"

"It is what you deserve, Willow. You deserve it – not because you always make the right choices and do the right things – none of us do. You deserve respect, kindness and love simply because you were born."

"Is that because to know me is to love me?!" purred Willow. Willow once again pounced on Mr. P with the vibrant joy of a freed spirit on her purr-fect journey to a sense of significance. When Peekaboo and Lucky saw the fun from afar, Peekaboo made a lively dash to join the pouncing. Lucky happily practiced his cart-wheeling to be part of the merriment.

Love is a powerful magnet!

Coaching Moments

You can trust that you are loved – greatly, deeply and widely!

To thrive, connect with the ever present, unfailing love of God.

To live boldly and to soar further than your wildest dreams:

- Be more conscious of your self-talk. *Words have the power to uplift or destroy. Which words will you choose? The choice is yours!*
- Living happier begins by speaking only blessings to oneself and others.
- Know that creating an atmosphere of genius and greatness begins with you. Identifying, replacing and affirming the truths and core beliefs you would rather have to live your genius are the first steps. Personal examples that changed my life dramatically are: Life is *for* me. *Everyone* is on my team for greatness. It's *just* a coaching moment – oops.
- List three ways your life would improve if you let people "off the hook" and stopped making others your source of acceptance, validation and self-worth. Consider meeting your own needs. Oh my goodness, you just soared higher, lighter and brighter!

Meet your own needs
to live your genius and greatness.

Living Your Joy

Mr. P was mesmerized with the sweet delicate scent of honeysuckle. Even heavenly scents were provided for his enjoyment. Mr. P grinned like a Cheshire cat who had eaten something very tasty.

> When he was fully present in the moment,
> bountiful gifts and abundance were everywhere.

Mr. P took a deep long breath as he understood that, when he was truly in the now, all his senses seemed more alive, intense and awake. He opened and entered the gates to paradise.

> *"I am living in the midst of plenty!"*

His senses felt a presence in the distance. It was Bondo waving an ecstatic furry paw. Even from afar, Mr. P was thrilled to see Bondo donning a full, glossy blond coat. There were no signs of stress patches. Once again the truth made visible with no bald patches of fur …

> *Change your thoughts,*
> *change your world – including your physical health.*

"Mr. P, how are you?" Bondo asked. His sincerity and joy touched Mr. P's essence.

"Better than ever, Bondo. Life is deliciously purr-fect! Your coat looks amazing, healthy and glowing."

"It's a miracle, P. My world immediately improved when I fully realized I am not accountable for the weather or another feline's happiness. Living up to the expectations of others had taken an incredible toll on my spirit, not to mention my fur coat.

> The heavy burden of shame, self-doubt and guilt lifted
> as I began to listen to the joy in my heart,
> to the truth of who I am."

Bondo joyfully continued sharing his learnings. "Changing old habits is hard, but not impossible! It hasn't been easy saying 'no.' I can still feel the heavy shroud of shame and guilt enveloping me at times. Then I choose to ask,

'Is this mine to do?'

My heart knows.

Each time I choose from love, my heart roars with delight. I become a radiating, pulsating center of joy. I feel I've won the cat treat lottery!"

Mr. P beamed with delight as he reflected on the truth.

Nothing is impossible with faith and better choices.

Mr. P gave Bondo the high-two paw. They both began emulating human football players doing the victory dance after completing a touchdown. They were here, happy and fully alive living in joy.

Coaching Moments

You can trust that living the joy in your heart is your unique purpose that reveals your perfect path for fulfilling your custom-made destiny.

You can live life more joyfully and energized by spending more time listening to the quiet still voice within instead of the screaming expectations and demands of others and the noise of the world.

You can skyrocket to the amazing joy-filled life you were meant to live if you:

- Ask yourself, *"Is this mine to do?"* when feeling the need to rescue or to save someone. Override the shame, guilt and voices of the past by immediately tuning into the quiet still voice within.
- Spend more time being still and just listening. If you are squeamish of the solitude, it is normal. I know I was. However it was in the silence that I found my authentic voice and purpose – my true self.
- Ask yourself, "Whose life and dreams am I living? *Why not live mine?"*
- Know that you are an original. Ignore the dream crushers. Have faith in you.

The world is awaiting your unique combination of gifts, talents and genius.

You Can Always Choose Again

It was a windy summer afternoon at Mr. P's cherished park. Mr. P was enthralled with the incredible visual display of colorful dancing kites with the long tails whipping through the cloudless blue skies. He delighted in the sounds of the giggles and shrills of the young children on the swings and merry-go-rounds.

Flying high like the kites was Peekaboo. Mr. P was in awe at the transformation of Peekaboo from a cowering cat to a poised feline springing to meet him.

"Mr. P, the affirmations worked! When I become afraid, I just say to myself ...

I am safe.

I am wanted.

I am divine!

As I shift my focus from the fear to God's love, I can breathe again. I gain strength, and the fear disappears as I sense the Creator's unconditional embrace of love and protection.

It really is a matter of focusing my thoughts.

My past does not have to equal my future."

Peekaboo hesitantly admitted, "I am worried though, Mr. P, that I will revert to old behaviors and once more become a timid scare-dy cat."

"I understand your concern, Peekaboo. Always remember …

You are far more powerful than you imagine.

The strength and love you feel in the presence of our Creator is *always* with you. There is no reverting to old patterns when you consciously stay connected. If you do get swept away by the hurtful memories and emotions of the past …

You can always choose to refocus your thoughts.

Every thought has power.

The love and the strength are only a thought away."

Mr. P lovingly added, "You are always moving forward even if it feels like you are plunging backwards. Continue to say your affirmations and consciously connect to the love that is always present. I promise the old patterns will decrease in frequency and duration." Peekaboo seemed relieved and relaxed with Mr. P's words of wisdom and encouragement.

Mr. P continued, "Peekaboo, there are times I *choose* to become invisible. I listen to my instincts and discern the sounds of my adversaries; I get to decide the best path to protect myself from harm either physically, verbally or emotionally.

I have learned to trust my instincts – to trust myself."

Peekaboo snuggled up to Mr. P as she meowed a song of peace from deep within her precious purr-riceless lovable soul. Her gleaming hazel eyes radiated contentment as she boldly danced away.

Mr. P was meowing the song in his heart of purr-fect peace and joy, and he reflected that ...

> *Words have the profound power to bless and to uplift*
> *or to curse and to destroy.*

Just as Mr. P had chosen once upon a time, Peekaboo had chosen to change her inner dialogue from self-reproach to self-love. With focus, courage and determination, Peekaboo had replaced her negative inner dialogue with constructive, encouraging words that nurtured her spirit.

With positive faith in her heart and the gift of choice, Peekaboo had discovered her unique song *and* her dancing paws, too!

Coaching Moments

You can trust that you possess within a one-of-a-kind song to sing and a dance waiting to be danced – no voice or rhythm required.

To live happier and to thrive, change your reality by changing your inner dialogue to one of love, encouragement and self-correction – not self-condemnation. There is a huge difference. Self-condemnation keeps you on the treadmill of "never enough." Self-correction and love lead to genius and greatness.

You can live life full throttle if you:

- Become conscious of *all* your internal dialogue. Take inventory as to whether your current words tend to be constructive and self-nurturing or filled with negativity and self-criticism.
- Keep a log or journal.
- Live consciously and shift to a positive, uplifting internal dialogue to live an extraordinary life.
- List seven ways you can create and foster more moments of delight in your life. Implement them now – no procrastinating.
- Create affirmations that express the life you *want* to live. As examples, the affirmations I say include: "I am joy-filled and Spirit-led." "I am relaxing and rejoicing." "The rest of my life *is* the best of my life."
- Say your affirmations out loud with enthusiasm and joyful expectations.

Anything is possible.
The choice is always yours!

Abra-Cat-Abra

More than a few days had passed since Mr. P had seen his red fiery furry friend, Scarlett. He often wondered how she was doing with her mood swings. Call it coincidence, synchronicity or providence, Mr. P spotted Scarlett. She was wobbling, as though dizzy from the ups and downs of her emotions. Their eyes met, and Mr. P was off running to be at her side.

"Scarlett, let me help you. You look dizzy."

"I am Mr. P. I can't seem to regain my balance. My head keeps spinning, my legs are shaky, my footing is unsure. I'm scared. Will you please share your medication with me?" she pleaded while batting her long, curly eyelashes.

"Scarlett, I would if I could. It has been years since I took my last pill." Scarlett collapsed and lost consciousness.

Mr. P was at her side when Scarlett opened her eyes. Her eyelashes looked heavier. "You're still here?"

"Where else would I be? Scarlett, I think it is time to hear the rest of the story." Mr. P dragged her limp body to rest in the shade of the big, leafy oak tree.

"The medication was a necessary start to clear my head, but it didn't change my lack of self-respect and self-esteem. I gained both with faith, focus and healthier choices." Scarlett's heart began to race.

Mr. P chose to reassure her by adding, "Not to worry, Scarlett.

It is a process that unfolds purr-fectly.

Everything is working for your good."

Scarlett's racing heart slowed as she listened to his calming words. She nestled further into the fallen oak leaves and grass. Mr. P continued.

"Deborah, the cat whisperer, helped a lot. I could say whatever I wanted, with no judgment from her, only a feeling of safety. We would laugh a lot, too. At times when I was recounting the cat-astrophes, she would laugh out loud. Of course, I initially got annoyed and upset, but then I could see the humor."

"Humor? You have got to be kidding, Mr. P."

"Oh, Scarlett, one day you'll be able to laugh at yourself, too, and the absurdity of it all. A lot of the pain and drama in my life was brought on by the energy I gave the sad moments of my past. I believe you are doing the same thing, Scarlett."

He gently continued, "Deborah taught me to recognize when I was overreacting to a minor situation. By recognizing my exaggerated reaction, I began to realize when I was attaching to the magnified painful memory I had kept alive by replaying and recounting the pain and injustice over and over again. Deborah suggested every time I would have an exaggerated reaction to ask myself the question,

'What memory is at the root cause of this reaction?'

When I learned and applied this technique, my life truly changed."

Scarlett, with a worried fur-roughed brow said, "Sounds good, Mr. P. What was the name of the meds you used to be on?"

"Paw-zac," Mr. P responded with kindness. "Let me walk you home, Scarlett."

"I would like that, Mr. P. I am so dreadfully tired. Tomorrow is another day."

Mr. P nodded in agreement that tomorrow was another day – a new beginning. He knew Scarlett's divine path would unfold purr-fectly.

Coaching Moments

You define you with every choice. Your DNA, your past or your environment do not define you. *You are far more powerful than you imagine.*

To live without the dizzying effects of drama, you need to consciously control your thoughts and emotions. Use the tremendous power of your mind, heart and spirit to live fearlessly at the core, resilient to external forces.

You can be resilient to external factors and skyrocket to a greater you if you:

- Become conscious of your reactions to current events – are they exaggerated or warranted with the present situation? *You can choose a different reaction, thought and belief. A change in thought and attitude changes everything.*
- Begin recognizing your triggers.
- Keeping a journal of the triggers and the situations to uncover underlying themes is powerful.
- Remember breathing and calmly affirming when triggered, "The earth did not stop with this." *Triggers are just friends in disguise.*
- Start using the tremendous power of your brain to create different thoughts and reactions that create a new story and tagline. Reframing, rewriting or tossing out the old script is life-changing.

You are the author and director of your life!

Hugs for Thugs

Mr. P spotted Bruiser doing his usual laps around the park. Scorching sun, pouring rain or sheets of sleet or heavy snow did not deter Bruiser from his daily workout. Bruiser was totally disciplined and never gave himself any slack. It would seem Bruiser was tougher on himself than he was on other cats.

Mr. P wanted to make amends with Bruiser since their last interaction. While Mr. P gave Bruiser a friendly wave on several occasions, the timing had not been right to approach Bruiser. Mr. P reflected that …

*Timing does count,
especially in sensitive matters.*

Today seemed like a good day to reconnect with Bruiser. There was a nice refreshing breeze, and the park was unusually quiet. When Mr. P saw Bruiser enter his cool-down lap, he approached.

"Hi, Bruiser. Okay if I join you for this lap?"

"No sweat off of me, Mr. P," Bruiser said coolly. "I do not plan to slow down. Understood?"

"Understood," replied Mr. P, thankful he was keeping pace. "Bruiser, I've wanted to talk to you about our last encounter."

Bruiser picked up the pace. Mr. P kept up and said, "Bruiser, all I want to say is that I am glad you were born."

Bruiser stopped dead in his tracks and said with a huff, "What did you say?"

Mr. P took a big huge gulp and repeated, "I am glad you were born."

Bruiser's bravado melted, his shoulders sank and he just looked at Mr. P. Mr. P returned the gaze with heartfelt reassurance.

"No one has ever told me they were glad I was born. Not anyone."

"Then it is time someone did," replied Mr. P. Bruiser stared at the ground so Mr. P could not see his vulnerability.

Mr. P continued, "For several lifetimes I thought life was hard and then you die. And because I was convinced that was the hand I was dealt, it became the hand I played. It seems I was always fighting to maintain a speck of who I was amidst the barrage of negativity from the litter I was born into as well as the environment. Just surviving was a good day back then for me, Bruiser."

Mr. P drove his perspective home by adding, "I was afraid of everything. Truth is, I believe a vast majority of us live our lives afraid. My fears included the fear of rejection, the fear of abandonment, the fear of not being good enough, the fear of failure and other fears too numerous to list. I lived life on the defensive. Life was a constant, continual fight. At times I was the bully; at other times I gave away my power and used guilt and shame to control others. My life was a mess!"

Bruiser nodded in agreement, his eyes fixated on the ground. "Go on, Mr. P."

"My world began to change with my new mom. She is forever saying, 'I love you, sweet P,' 'I am so glad you were born,' 'God must really love me for you to have landed on my doorstep.' I came to the realization the Creator must really love me, too, to have her as a mom. She was my last chance to have a home. I was already nine years old.

As I changed my thoughts, my beliefs began to change.

Everything changed for the better and greater.

Change your thoughts to change your world is my motto!

Bruiser, I can assure you, you are loved, too – deeply and dearly, just as you are."

Bruiser was speechless. He was sure the tears would flow and would ruin his image if he spoke or even meowed. Mr. P continued. "Bruiser, you are very bright and disciplined. I want you to use those gifts for your good. Start by affirming continuously …

I am a good cat.

I am invaluable.

Life is for me.

I stop all forms of fighting.

As you say this to yourself, Bruiser, imagine receiving unconditional love. Imagine the feeling of being wrapped in the arms of pure acceptance and safety. The habit of fighting is engrained, Bruiser. So each time you feel the boxing gloves going on, the laces tightening, breathe and refocus on the affirmations. You *will* prevail."

"Thanks for the vote of confidence, Mr. P, and for taking the time to approach me. I need time to think. We'll talk again soon."

As Bruiser slowly walked away, Mr. P reflected as he often did how all creatures are more alike than different. Regardless of markings or origins, it would seem everyone needed to know and feel …

I am wanted.

I matter.

I am loved.

The truth as Mr. P had come to understand was that …

Everyone is wanted, does make a difference and is loved.

We are all significant pieces of the puzzle called life.

Coaching Moments

You can trust your worth and significance are established. You are breathing.

To thrive, stop fighting and start living the truth of who you are. Even if you don't believe in a loving God, He still believes in you.

You can skyrocket to the abundant, greater life and touch the stars if you:

- Select five people to express, "I am glad you were born," with a smile and a simple gesture of kindness such as a hug or a twinkle in your eyes.
- List the beliefs and labels that are holding you hostage, and then implement a tactical game plan to set yourself free. As a point of reference, several research studies have concluded that human infants are born with only two fears. The two fears are: the fear of falling and the fear of loud noises. All other fears are man-made and self-imposed. Ask yourself, *"What 'mind-made' fears are keeping me fighting?"*
- Answer truthfully, "What color and size are my boxing gloves?"
- Reflect and consider, "What is the worst thing that would happen if I stepped out of the boxing ring and hung up my gloves?"
- Understand that proving that you can overcome a challenge or meet an opportunity builds self-respect. Proving you have worth, however, is at the basis of most self-defeating, dysfunctional behaviors.

Believe and think greater to live greater.

Here and Happy

Mr. P was ecstatic to be at his beloved park. It had thundered and stormed the last few days as life itself could do at times. During the darkness and dreariness, Mr. P knew the result would be good. He knew in the depths of his heart and soul that …

God was good all the time.

The sun was always there.

The darkness was only temporary.

The rain and showers were gifts to nourish the thirsty earth and to help things grow.

"Stunning" was the only word that captured the beauty before him. There was the most lavishly-colored rainbow Mr. P had ever seen stretching and glimmering across the endless blue sky. All creatures were celebrating a new dawn, a new beginning. The merriment was contagious. The contrast of the cardinals' ravishing red feathers against the landscape made it appear more luscious and inviting. Miraculously, a white dove appeared, or was it an albino pigeon?

Mr. P's rough tongue licked his thin lips. He chuckled. "We'll call it a dove." He had learned that …

*Life is full of miracles
when you choose to see them.*

Mr. P fell on his four white chunky paws in gratitude and bliss. To be fully awake to all there was in every moment was heaven on earth. No more fighting, struggling or resistance …

Simply connection, trust and love.

Even with Mr. P's countless "wrong" choices, he ended up in the right place.

Mr. P felt he was an integral part of the whole, as was everyone, from the Hoovers to the Esperanzas. Mr. P understood that …

While personalities were diverse
and at different stages of love,
all were created in the image and likeness of God.

Mr. P smiled as he observed the newcomers to the park. He was sure they had much to teach him about trust, playing well with others and thriving.

Another wave of gratitude washed over Mr. P, tears of joy and happiness flowed freely down his furry fat cheeks at the purr-fection and beauty of it all. Mr. P raised his front paws to the vast, limitless sky giving praise and rejoicing …

"I was created on purr-pose for a purr-pose!

I am a purr-riceless treasure!

I am glad to be me!

Now is the best now I have ever known!

Yeah for me!"

Epilogue – Fur Now

Bondo, donning a stunning blond fur coat, is founder and CEO of "Joy *Your* Way" Park Resource Centers throughout the metroplex.

Bruiser is crusin' the park with a glow-in-the-dark bright yellow happy faces collar that pushes the giggles button of everyone. The collar lays against a fluffy fur neck following his cat-too removal process.

Chen connects millions to the Creator's presence with his award winning "Cat-Chi Program – Keeping Mind, Body and Spirit in Purr-fection."

Harvey, wearing his lively green "I AM Harvey" t-shirt, is a highly sought cat-noter and speaker. His upbeat, positive message, "Sad to Glad – Declawed to Delighted" is like refreshing water to the thirsty, weary spirit.

Hoover unknowingly entertains park goers by his perpetual worship at the cathedral of St. Saks and himself.

Esperanza was thankfully discovered by a Tail-Tube fan. Her adoring public calls her "Grace in Action" due to her joyful and reassuring message, "God loves you exactly where you are."

Luci disappeared mysteriously one dark, stormy night amidst innuendos and rumors, never to be seen again.

Lucky loves his unofficial designation as park greeter. His winning attitude and cheerful disposition gave him the courage and creativity to be the first pole vaulting, cart-wheeling, three-legged feline wonder.

Peekaboo pinches herself and raises her paws in praise daily for her good fortune. Peekaboo skyrocketed to success as a kitty rock star with her Grammy Award winning singles, "Be Visible" and "Simply Because."

Mr. P is living "happily ever after" in the moment. He marvels at the trillion of miracles each breath signifies. He is having a delicious, scrumptious time paw-ing his riveting, fur-raising, belly-chuckling memoirs, *Here and Happy on No Meds*.

Scarlett is a full-swaying, sassy, sensational comedienne. She is putting the fun back in dys-fun-ctional with her one act show, "Purring on Paw-zac."

Willow is a glowing example of finding your inner kitty. No longer an approval junkie, she has embraced her divine heritage. She radiates self-worth and confidence, which come from her inner belief she is purr-riceless, precious and greatly loved.

Dare to be a Greater You!

I believe *Happy in Spite of People* will bring out your inner greatness so that you can live an extraordinary life regardless of the personalities in your workplace, home or community. Understanding and applying the book's people genius insights and skills will give you favor, both in business and in life.

Favor? Yes! My extensive business experience – ranging from leading an Exxon service station profit center in the 1970s to serving as a trusted Fortune 500 company consultant and greatness coach to thousands today – has shown me that *individuals with a high degree of social awareness and people skills are always in demand.* Harnessing the power of people genius keeps the doors open to greater opportunities regardless of external factors. *People naturally help and promote people they like, respect and trust!*

The secret to being happy in spite of people is realizing no personality is "wrong." We are all multi-faceted. Everyone is on our team for greatness. We are all valuable in this amazing galaxy we call "life." Choosing the people-friendly mindsets offered in *Happy in Spite of People* will skyrocket the quality of your relationships, your work *and* your life to the amazing heights for which you were created. I am personally grateful for all the "cats in the park." They make life interesting and meaningful. And they are the reason that coaching clients to higher levels of *excellence and greatness through and with people* has become my passion and purpose.

Greatness is unleashed as we realize that life is for us and that our choices – not our past – define us. There are no failures, simply opportunities to choose again. We keep moving forward, knowing that sometimes wrong directions lead us to the right place. It's the place where we live and love *our* authentic life to the max and achieve lasting success by enriching the lives of others in *our* unique way.

The world is waiting for your genius!

Let love reign!

Dare to be a greater you!

*May your roots go down
deep into the soil
of God's marvelous love.
And may you have
the power to understand,
as all God's people should,
how wide, how long,
how high and how deep his love really is.*

— Ephesians 3:17-18

Unstuck and Unlimited

Stuck? Get Ellen, *Your* Chief Energizing Officer! Always energizing, creative and practical, she removes roadblocks to create breakthrough solutions for pressing problems or innovative approaches to unique opportunities. With an independent global perspective and expertise spanning 17 industries, Ellen provides the strategic, business and people acumen you need to break out of "stuck and limited" circumstances, both personally and professionally.

Ellen's warmth, keen intuition and competence rich in business, educational and personal experience are your guide to achieving the extraordinary. Her empowering services and customized solutions include:

- ❖ People Genius Leadership and High Octane Coaching
- ❖ Dynamic Consulting for Dynamic Times
- ❖ Captivating *Dare to be a Greater You* Keynotes and Programs
- ❖ Supercharged Conflict Management and Resolution for Strategic Turnarounds
- ❖ Rocket Fuel Facilitation that Drives Trust and Results

Explore the exhilarating possibilities for igniting passion, fueling engagement and unleashing *your* potential today.

Connect with Ellen Castro, *Chief Energizing Officer*
Ellen@EllenCastro.com
www.EllenCastro.com

Need a real-world blueprint and toolkit for living courageously regardless of external forces? Buy Ellen's *Spirited Leadership: 52 Ways to Build Trust,* recipient of the International Latino Award for "Best Self-Help Book." Please visit www.EllenCastro.com for information.

Subscribe to *Igniting Greatness Coaching Moments by Ellen* at www.EllenCastro.com/ellen-castro-newsletter.htm.

Live unstuck, unlimited and uplifted by following Ellen on www.twitter.com/IgnitingSpirit.

Break through to a Greater You!

You are meant for Greatness, period!

Live from the Possibilities with Ellen!

Change your thoughts, change your world.

You were created on purpose for a purpose.

Your choices define you.

You are far more powerful
than you imagine.

The only failure is giving up.

Everyone is on your team for greatness – no exceptions.

You are meant for greatness!

www.ingramcontent.com/pod-product-compliance
Lightning Source LLC
Chambersburg PA
CBHW061444040426
42450CB00007B/1200